AFTER OCTOBER

To Val
with best wishes
Jim
14/6/03

AFTER OCTOBER

by

JAMES BURCH

Phygtyles Press
5, Bridle Lane
Downham Market
Norfolk PE38 9QZ

First published in 2003
PHYGTYLES PRESS,
5, Bridle Lane,
Downham Market,
Norfolk, PE38 9QZ

e-mail: phygtylespress@eidosnet.co.uk

Printed by King's Lynn Printers

ISBN: 0-9545053-0-1

CONTENTS

PART ONE

BEFORE

PART TWO

AFTER

INTRODUCTION

Of the seventy poems in this volume Thea, who features in them all, saw only the first twenty, the ones written during her lifetime. I feel uncomfortable about this. The near fifty years we spent together are directly represented only by those twenty poems, and all too few of these are celebratory, with the others dwelling on doubts, rows, partings, illness and ageing, whereas the three and a half years since she died have yielded more than twice as many. It is as though whilst alive she was part of my life, but in death became all of it. Perhaps, from being too busy and content to write much poetry, I then became, for a while, too wretched to do much of anything else.

I am also uncomfortable with the fact that so many of the poems are more about me, the whingeing survivor, than about Thea, who, with so much about which she could have complained, fought so bravely and cheerfully to the end. If the poems are good enough, I hope I will be excused. I especially hope that all those who knew Thea will find in at least some of these poems some features of her that they will recognise. She is there, in all of them, if you look hard enough. All of the later poems draw whatever strength and authenticity they may have from those many good years we had together.

In the spring of 1985, Thea, who had been experiencing increasingly bothersome difficulties with her breathing, and feeling generally unwell, was diagnosed as having asthma. Hardly had the treatment of this condition begun than a closer look at the X-rays raised the possibility of a tumour on one of her lungs. Further examinations confirmed this. Whilst awaiting surgery, infection from a tooth spread to one of her heart-valves. This in itself was a life-threatening condition, and it was fortunate that, because she was already being closely monitored, it was detected early. The infection was cleared up, but the valve was left damaged. The operation to remove part of one lung was traumatic but successful, and there was no recurrence of the cancer. However, as we subsequently learned, she also had severe emphysema affecting both lungs.

All of these factors combined to leave her with permanent severe breathing difficulties, which, year by year, slowly worsened. She was unable to complete an accountancy course she had been following, or to return to work. She was very easily tired by any physical exertion, and soon had to submit to being pushed in a wheel-chair when out and about. But she continued to enjoy life, and contrived to enhance greatly the lives of others. Cooking, shopping, children, grand-children and great grand-children, friends, holidays, reading, watching TV and some gentle gardening helped to fill her days.

On September 22nd 1999, whilst preparing a meal and entertaining a visiting friend, she suffered sudden and severe chest pains. An ambulance was summoned and she was rushed into hospital. The better of her lungs had collapsed, with near fatal results. However, once diagnosed and receiving treatment, she soon looked and felt more comfortable, and we were told that there were excellent prospects of a complete recovery. This episode is the subject of the poem, 'Late September.'

After nearly a week in hospital, and within a day or so of being discharged as fit to return home, a complication set in. Surgical emphysema was the name they gave it. Initially, the medical staff were reassuring that this too, though alarming, could be dealt with successfully. However, after a day of considerable discomfort, during which, nevertheless, Thea remained cheerful, optimistic and reassuring towards the rest of us, it became increasingly clear that her condition was worsening and, in spite of the considerable efforts of the doctors and nurses, early in the morning of October 1st she died. The first poem in Part 2, 'The Dangling Man', was written a month or so later, and is about that last night of Thea's life. All of the poems which follow, with just a few exceptions, are in the order in which they were written.

ACKNOWLEDGEMENTS

My grateful thanks to Carolyn, Nick, Sarah, Pearl, Ned, Anne, Diana, Bill Wall, Jo and all those others, family and friends, who have read some or all of these poems, as they were written over the years. Being a stubborn bugger, I would of course have gone on writing them anyway, but their interest, appreciation, considerate criticism and encouragement were a huge bonus.

Thanks are also due to the King's Lynn Writers' Circle, Downham Pub Poets, Fakenham Shed Poets, King's Lynn Centre Poets, West Acre Theatre, The King's Lynn Festival, Wells-next-the-Sea Poetry Festival and the Ostrich at Castle Acre, all of which provided venues in which the poems could be read to an audience. The ride was sometimes bumpy, but always helpful.

Thanks as well to the magazines Breathe, Poetry Monthly, The Penniless Press, Poetry Review and the London Evening Standard in which, at various times, some of these poems have appeared, to Rita Kearton for advice on cover design and to Tony and Andy Hoare of King's Lynn Press Limited for his help in getting this volume printed.

To
Thea

BEFORE

Valentine.

Listen!
When we meet,
Let us by all means
Be discreet,
But let us kiss.

A common thing,
Which,
Had I panache,
We
Might already be
Enjoying.

But,
Though socially inept,
Let me not indefinitely
In this state of kisslessness
Be kept.

Let the next item on our agenda
Be, to end a
Situation flattening,
In which,
Unpetuous and unrash,
Kisses are not happening.

Let us start afresh
And, at ever shorter intervals,
Meet, press lips, and part.
Greet, and kiss, and part,
And kiss, and part,
And kiss, repeatedly,
Sweetheart.

Just-Good-Friendship.

We exchanged
What was meant to be
A comradely kiss
In friendship,
But
The venture turned out strange.
I felt
Each
Separate
Molecule
In my body
Rearrange.
Each bone,
Joint,
Muscle-fibre,
Gland
And gristle,
Sang.
Skin temperature
Seemed to rise.
Yet still we deemed it safe,
This enterprise.
Bold credits and titles
Next began to roll.
What fanfares then!
New visions of our world
As seen from space,
Its rivers and forests,
Mountains
And Great Wall,
And wreaths of stars,
And clouds humped softly on and on
To the edge of sight,
And black and shiny night,
Bright seas,
Beaches,
Rocks,
And towering cliffs,

And,
After this,
More thoughtful now,
We moved
Into our second kiss.

Daydreams

You ask me what I hope for?

I hope
That one day
I will wake to find myself looking at you
And, having blinked,
And looked again,
And blinked again,
And rubbed in sharp surprise
My widening eyes,
Will, between cool sheets,
Upon white pillows,
See your face still turned,
Looking towards my face,
And will know that it is true.

And that,
After this calm, browsing gaze,
We slowly move,
With careful confidence,
And tongues ablaze,
And nerves a-scream,
And gathering pace,
Back to the fierce entanglements
Of my dream.

Falling.

Could you always tell
When I told lies?
As we flicked
To and fro
Our words about love,
And caught them lightly,
But with careful eyes?
Sometimes
I thought you could.
Panics would drench me.
I'd watch you see the drops
And speculate
And ponder such displays.
Watch your eyes
Move,
As old evidence
Gathered new patterns
Under your inward gaze.
Patter
Would falter,
Bold words
Fade out in sighs,
Their cover blown.
And now
The cool deceiver
Out-countenanced lies,
His secret,
Sad surrender
Known and known.
Your certain knowledge
Growing by the minute,
That when he idly talks of love,
He fears he means it.

Mornings with T.

I drink my tea,
Sipping
From the small warm cup,
Slowly,
While I wait.

She arrives.
We kiss,
Undress,
Do our various
Tender,
Usual things,
Then drink more tea,
Together.

The wall behind her
Delicately bare,
We sit
In silence,
The empty, endless day
Joyously
Brimming.

Birthday

My gloved hand upon your shoulder,
Our floating glances lost upon the water,
Sauntering on shallow steps,
Pulling close together from the cold,
Sharing thoughts
Of me,
Of you,
Starting to walk another chill, grim winter through.

Planks and twigs
And sodden pages,
Soaked through withThames
From stream and sewer,
In every drop
Through all these waters,
By Hungerford and Waterloo,
Traces, no doubt, of me,
Traces of you.

Once,
I remember,
When your bulge showed clearly,
You cried as we walked
Near Brixton market,
Eyes looked from buses,
Fingers appeared,
Lips moved
Miming undubbed messages
For our deaf eyes to see,
Whispers of you,
Whispers of me.

Tonight,
With our urgent headlamp beams
Bright,
But,

Shortened by fog,
Against us,
You hang from the window
To report upon kerbs or catseye gleams.

Turning,
Between labours,
To speak,
Briefly our breath-clouds mingle,
Visibly,
Like spirits
We have quick privilege to see,
Minglings of you,
Minglings of me.

Hospital doors and walls,
Beds and bowls and linen,
Breaking of waters,
Gas and pain and air.
A small squadged face,
Mauve,
Starved blue,
But features unfolding now,
With glimpses, I swear, of me,
Glimpses of you.

Into the morning,
Greeting the cold,
Gulping great breaths of therapeutic fog,
Feeling the world spin back beneath my shoe,
Barking benignly
At an early dog,
Walking
And wisely smirking,
Gratefully me,
Grateful for you,
And grateful too
For our new me-and-you,
Joining and journeying with us now
This fine, warm, joyful winter through.

Crash Course in Accounting.

It's hot, you say, in Nottingham today.
Windows collecting heat,
Desks beating it back and back about the room.
Pub-lunched with somebody, you say.
You do not mention whom.
The cramming is tough but good, the day is long.
Your desk companion is a lady from Hong Kong.

Problems and problems yesterday, you say.
The phone exploding and the boss at bay.
Twenty four hours of studenthood and midnight oil,
The world, unwatched, comes swiftly to the boil.

The news is through, I say, about my trip.
I hear the muscles moving in your lip.
One month, one week.
We feel we must, but find we cannot, speak.

Audiograms shape the cobwebs on the wall.
I marvel that a voice can be so small.
The lines, you see, are thin,
And time comes swirling in.

I move to stay.
Travel to keep my way.
Change to be as I am,
To help to bear the heat of Nottingham.

Parting

It was not during the war,
But after,
That I learned about parting.

Then,
I was the sad-eyed,
Fringe-faced,
Raincoat-docketed,
Quaint,
All-purpose,
Wondering boy,
Who studied London's burning.
Looked skyward at the silver fish,
And watched them fight,
And falling.
Heard news of armies, towns and ships,
Marched flags with pins across a map,
Saw bodies scattered in a park,
And worried about homework.

Seems fifteen thousand years ago,
A Babylonian picture-show,
Some suffering,
Some courage too,
But fifteen thousand years B.Y.
Before you,
My dear,
Before you.

Now,
If I scratch at memory,
Pick at the scars upon my brain,
Reverberate old circuitries,
Release old hurts to hurt again,
There is one scene,
It will not hold,

But comes
And slips and slips and slips..

Not planes, or tanks, or bombs, or blood,
Or refugees in tired flood,
Or guards with whips,
But....

Woburn pavements,
Woburn Square,
And you beside some railings there,
Forlorn in the taxi's window frame,
Diminishing with every wave,
And both our faces paling.

Journeys.

My dear,
Whilst I have been away,
During the time we have been apart,
I have been reading a book,
By some Robertsons
I believe,
About children
Going into hospital.

They cry
Distressingly at first,
But later,
Become
Delicately calm,
And cope.

But,
Later still,
Cannot quite manage
Rapture
Or reunion
With their home.

I read too
Of parents,
Full of great love
And pain,
Poised nervously,
Ready to swamp,
Hungry to clasp,
Desperate to laugh,
Or cry,
But fearful of repulse,

All taking time,
A long, sad time,
In testing,

Teasing,
And not trusting.

How will it be with us
When I return?
How will we cope?

How have we coped
In our poor cots
Apart?

What shell have we developed,
Shield,
Or crutch?

How will it be?

One in full flood,
The other frozen fast?
One quick to pounce,
The other one aghast?
Be both polite and careful at first touch?
Or fierce?
Or drunk?
Or mild?

And which of us the parent,
Which the child?

Shadows.

You travel the world
By boat and plane.
I stay at home
Or take the train.

I seek adventure
In each pausing face,
And tempt the world to visit, nightly,
In your place.

Your tall, trailed vapour
Stands quite still.
My stillness moves.
The space between us fills...
Rippled with love.

Festival in Penang.

I watch men walk
On burning coals
To reach,
Sedate,
At speed,
The milky trough.
I hear it,
Hissing,
Cool their miracle.

Others
Impale their flesh
With hooks
To tug small carts.
Or slice their tongues,
Bloodless
At touch of ash.

Led to the temple,
Priests strike them,
Fast and sharp,
To break the spell.

Intelligence returns.
They leave the dance.

Your eyes carry
Resolved oblivion of pain.
You narrow your nose
To dodge the puff of dust.
You know it is disease which keeps us pure,
And walk, entranced,
Beyond the reach of cure.

Ridge of Pressure.

All seemed clear an hour ago.
Trees bore moss on one side only.
Streams pursued a tidy point of compass.
The sun shone steadily upon our sundial backs.
Our feet were well informed,
Our palms touched warm
And, at each touch of thigh,
Knowledge most carnal
Grew like a bruise between us,
When,
At a word,
Our slithering, stubbing toes
Conjured petulant rains,
Which broke and burst our ground,
Leaving us lost in treeless cloudscape,
Bloodless and lustless,
Fearful of gangrene.

Tested to Destruction.

The matter was trivial,
But we had pushed too far.

Through the dark windscreen,
Along new distances,
I see cold,
Feel quiet,
Sense solitariness in rooms.

A brink,
And beyond the brink,
Hardness.
Matters are certain,
Brisk and firm.
Actions count.
Words echo and echo
Till they are heard.
Things are set down.

So,
'Verily, verily,'
You say unto me,
'The pea'
'Has finally'
'Worked its way'
'To the top of the mattress.'

And,
From the toadish nodding
Of my head,
You see
I agree.

Nightwatch.

His walk took him past lilac,
Roses in bush,
Through deep wet grass.

It was late. He came to see her pass.

His gaze took in trees in a line
And shallow hills,
Distant, chimneyed smoke.

Nearer scenes might choke.

The road showed movement.

Earth, crouched at his feet, surprised him.
All else dissolved to shadow,
Each tree a fleeing wraith,

But morning would show their faith.

Leaving at evening,
Her detail nearly too small to see,
The eye cornered her flight.

Her shifts revealed, then took her from, his sight.

Echoes.

There is a T.V. trick,
To round the plot,
Instead of the denouement,
Full and pat,
To freeze the scene,
Then jump through many another frozen shot,
A door half-shut, a mouth about to scream,
A foot upon a glass about to crack,
A clock-face caught mid-tick,
A feline prowl, at pause,
All these kaleidoscoped,
Converted to a theme.

Now that the great dramas of our love are past,
It seems to me a truer image is the holophrast.
Each single, simple splinter tells it all.
Has every angle,
Tactile and fragrant,
Visual,
Full of sound.
So,
Though that frightful hazard smashed us down,
Each fracture only multiplied our truth.

One ticket, photo, comb or card,
That coat, this cup, that rose, this lawn, that bush,
A tone, or posture, touch, or tug, or push,
Encapsulates our story, told in full,
Disrupts variety,
Makes old Heraclitus out a fool,
And raises shivers of eternity.

Case-notes.

Why do you keep saying words?
Pricking my vigil?
None of them make sense.
All of them promise sense.
"I am afraid of the dark."
"I will fall down."
"If only we had another two per cent."
"It is full of holes."
"Anyone can buy one."

What is the meaning of a fever
That it chooses,
"Why am I hot?"
"He is a lovely boy."
"Anyone can get one if they pay."
"I will fall down."?

Why does your breath not settle?
Why will it not settle into sleep?
Why do you talk?
"I am so tired."
"Can I have ice?"
"I have to watch him every minute."
"You only have to ask."

Why do I have to listen?
Why am I full of holes?
If I get another two per cent,
Will I be able to pay?
Who is it she is watching every minute?
Is she truly, truly afraid of the dark?
When will I fall down?

Nightscapes.

Your knees are hot and sharp.
How loud your breath.
Sleep lurks somewhere there
Between you and this page,
But will not go or come.

Sheets full of corrugations
And of crumbs.
Feet,
Creep-cramped and blanket-trapped,
Scream for release and air.

I remember the crowded shelter,
Lit by exploding shells.
My then boy's body bursting too
With stifled twitches.
Each move a border incident
Unleashing swift reprisals,
Massive retaliations,
States of bed-alert.

But I remember other nights,
Our unclothed flesh sponge-like with desire,
And skins a creeping fire,
Adventure in each crease, and fold, and touch,
And every breath incendiary and fresh,
And elbows, toe-nails, paunch and nicotine,
All in the screech and shrapnell-storm clean gone,
And, full of surging sleep,
Our fogged, smeared, bitten, shell-shocked, crude, dishevelled ears,
And tattered lips,
And smouldering eyes,
Converged in loud rejoicing cries,
And tired smiles,
To reach All Clear.

View from the Uplands

The path we followed was mostly marked,
Compact with previous feet,
Hiding at times in marsh or gullies,
But emerging later, shaking off splashes or flints.

The ground we covered changed,
Pastures and stiles,
Hazards and havens,
Felled trees, cracked walls, a fruiting bush,
Rivers that dragged and churned,
Cool, flickering beaches and abandoned foam.

Along the way,
We built a house,
Furnished with whim and thought,
Scratchful of treasure,
Pine-walled, and carpeted, and clean.
We had snaps and tapes, and good sharp talk,
And padded about soft-foot.

The path we left continues,
Climbs to a skyline crammed with unvisited peaks,
Deep valleys, secret and soft.
When moon or sun are right,
Lakes wink at our windows,
And the far forests yearn and yearn
For their faltered pilgrims.

Babes in the World.

Snow,
Wind-thinned,
In steady, squirting jets,
Sieved through pine and spruce.

They felt their snow-skins grow,
Crack and re-set,
Lungs lose use.

Driven, fine sky-fragments
Pushed at mouth and nose without relief,
Encrusted eyes.

Their dogged, last defence,
Stunned by disbelief,
They dropped in slow surprise.

And tired and strangely warm,
And curled and clasped,
They drifted into sleep
And drew last breath
Just breadcrumb's-throw from home.

Touchdown.

Moment to moment,
Through window-taps,
Fire-snaps,
Jokes,
Strokes,
Tiredness
And tremor,
You find me,
Find your way to me.

Passage to passage,
Glass ghosting,
Breasting through tall grass,
Hips swayed,
Sea swathed.

Pan visioned,
I watch your approach.

In sleep,
In speculation,
Dream-doodling,
Guardless at thought,
Open,
In you fly.

I smile,
Smile at your touch.

Late September

They knew things that I didn't know,
The ambulance men,
As,
After the oxygen,
The inhalers,
The doctor,
The stretcher,
We sped through the night,
Past sad signposts,
Past dark, dripping trees,
Hunched hedges,
Hazard lights flashing,
Me following,
They pulling ahead,
Rushing you straight through the doors,
Me left behind,
Searching for parking.

They knew things I didn't,
As they waited to catch me,
As I moved forward, fearful,
To tease out their news.

They told me some of it.
The surgeon had seen you,
He now knew the trouble,
Had now diagnosed it,
Was waiting for X-rays,
But was sure they could cure it.
Said how close it had been,
But was sure you would live.

But still,
As they led me
Away from Reception,
Away from the others,
To a small quiet room,

And sat watchfully with me,
Plied me with tea,
There was still something they knew
That I didn't know.

That,
After the fears,
The dark, lonely ride,
Bright hospital lights,
The good-sounding news,
Relief would expand
To bloat like a duvet,
And explode through my head
As a torrent of tears.

27

28

29

AFTER

The Dangling Man

Behold the dangling man.
His feet above the ground.
His fingers at his throat.
He screams without a sound.

Behold the dangling man.
His fingers at his throat.
In stifling winter air,
He wears no winter coat.

Behold the darkened wood,
Its darkened branches bare,
To hold the dangling man,
And starve his lungs of air.

Behold there is no wood,
No branch, no knot, no rope,
But still the dangling man,
His tissues starved of hope.

His fingers clutch his throat.
His arms entwine his head.
His eyes afraid to look
Upon the busy bed.

The creatures of the night
They pounce and prick and pound,
Ignore the dangling man,
And work without a sound.

They put their knives away,
And meet his searching eye,
Invite the dangling man
To say a last goodbye.

He heard the danger call
And said goodbye, to hope.
His feet sought out the ground.
His hands flew to the rope.

Now from the corner dark,
His arms about his head,
His face a streaming veil,
He moves towards the bed.

Coroner and nurses,
Be gentle as you can,
With your deceased, my darling,
And pity the dangling man.

Walking with Visions.

A life of clear detail
Has become heavy with obscure profundities.

I ponder how species
Arose, like bubbles,
To burst and disappear,
We study their death-masks in the rocks,
And how our lives
Can come and go,
Just simply go.

A birth is registered,
A diet planned,
Calories counted,
Measurements taken down,
Clothes slightly altered,
Dosages judged.

A life is a thing of infinite pains,
But then,
Just ends.

There is no other room,
No better place,
No life beyond.

We happen,
Then we stop.
We do not go on.
It is only the stopping that goes on,
And on.

You will not come back.
We will not meet again.

I remember how we used to walk,
A holiday outing,

And then go home.

Take children to the shops
To buy and save,
Then take them home.

Rush furiously to work,
Meet at King's Cross
And then
Go, talking, home.

Have days of crises,
Rows, adventures,
Disappointments,
Tears,
But then go home.

Travel
Or visit friends,
And then go home.

Face injury,
Illness,
Surgery,
Deep hurt,
But then,
Tenderly, with care,
Go, fondly, home.

My feet tread mud.
Memories shriek through the hedge.
I avoid the gaze of other walkers.
My face feels curiously clenched.
My skin, creased paper, in the cold.

I walk with visions,
And then,
Alone,
Go home.

Most Days

Most days I cry.
Each day alone
Seems long.
Days of quick, lively fun
Far gone.

Nothing alarms me
Now,
With nothing left
To fear.
Your absence is so near.

Most days I cry,
Sometimes a lot.
You were my heroine,
But now
I've lost that plot.

Most nights I cry.
Most times no-one hears.
Some thoughts, they always make me cry.
Thoughts about thoughts
Bring tears about tears.

Any Advance on Nothing

When you lived,
There were days when your muscles
Still craved the exercise
Your lungs could no longer fuel,
When your heart needed to pump
More than the faulty valve allowed,
When your limbs begged for their old powers
To dance, to swim, to walk.

Toning tables were the answer.
Tuning tables perhaps,
Fine tuning,
Nursing, coaxing, teasing,
With delicate, passive, machine-led movement,
Keeping life flowing,
Preserving strength,
In your weakened body.
Lying in turn on each of seven tables,
Responding to each of fourteen different
Whirls and turns,
Tilts or lifts,
A kind of bliss,
Virtual exertion,
Not quite a quick-step
Or your parlour-piece Charleston,
But, a big advance on nothing.

Now that you do not live,
It is I who go through the motions.
Going out and coming in,
Sitting and standing,
Talking and falling quiet.
Eating, breathing, waiting,
To see if signs of life return,
Or any advance on nothing.

Especially Neat

Especially,
You were neat.
Your naked back
A miracle of line and curve.
To look at often seemed enough,
But never was.
Nor just to touch.
To trace, with electric finger tips,
Those shapes,
Was to stir a cauldron.
Tactile temptations are the worst,
The best.
A week before I had been seriously mad,
Staring at walls,
Watching days slip by,
Listening at doors,
Imagining lives that were real,
A premature ghost,
Awaiting death, to be born.
Then,
Through chance,
With talk,
By smiles
And luck
And solemn, mutual scheming,
I was in your bed,
Face to face,
Looking and tasting,
Feasting,
Aghast at your perfection,
Confronted by fate's kindness,
Force fed with dreams.
You were love's learning curve.
Those dear sweet breasts,
That tiny waist,
Those tiny pulsing feet.....
Many are the other things you were

Or became,
But,
At today's special haunting,
What I recall,
On tip-toe, peeping thought,
Is that,
Especially,
You were neat.

What Kind of Pain?

Looking at old photos
Puts a knife through the heart.
I try to turn away
But,
The pages turn.
A fresh wound every day.

Should images of laughter,
Loving glances,
And so-tender touch,
So precious now,
Hurt so much?

What kind of pain is this?
Moments which surface now
Have often long been lost.
Recovered joy incurs
Discovered pain as cost.

Did we live too much on the frontiers of our lives,
Defeating dragons,
Tenderly tough,
Too many good years slipping past,
Did not remember, did not savour them enough?

We made no choice.
We simply lived our lives.
Each picture holds its pain.
Redundant fingers turn the page again.

Who's the Loser?

A magpie struts the lawn,
Hoping for some bread.
Our schedules do not match.
He flies away, unfed.

I later break a loaf,
And throw some pieces down.
The Magpie doesn't come.
He had a date in town.

One Hand Clapping

You were your best with babies.
Good with many things
But, at your very best with them.

The small, warm body resting upon your arm,
Your arm resting upon your body,
Both of you looking out,
Then looking in.

That confident, loving smile.
'This is the best life gets,'
It seems to say.

One small hand applauds.

Carry on Regardless?

What is happening to my face?

Before,
Was continual traffic,
Jokes,
Comments,
Groans,
Silly voices, silly looks,
Memories,
Questions,
Answers,
Peak hours and troughs,
Worries,
Manoeuvres,
Serious plans,
All peppered with puns, quips, laughter,
Qualms.

A face, in all of its time,
Unconsciously conscious
Of your regard,
Now stretched and pinched.

Not sea or sand,
Sparkling or shifting,
Empty as glass,
An abandoned runway,
Scorched,
But silent.

Was You

It's not that I was unprepared,
Or gave the matter little thought,
Or carelessly, in callow youth,
Religious consolation spurned,
Or felt, by all my goodly deeds,
I'd somehow huge exemptions earned,
Or feared the onrush of the dark,
Or devil's breath,
Or arctic cold,
Or could not understand the role,
Death plays in life's short mystery.
It is not in death's contract
To advertise his last approach,
He touches every citizen,
And favours none,
Nor heeds reproach.
Amongst my baggage,
Constantly,
My readiness was kept in view.
I was not smart, or scared, or brave,
Just braced to meet a fate I thought I knew.
But curse I will,
Complain I will,
Destroy I would,
And burn I would,
And bleed I must,
And scream I must,
And howl and weep and hide I shall,
For it was you, was you, was you,
Was you, was you, was you, was you.

Castaway Kid

Some of the fragments I remember.

A garden picnic.
Marooned with you on a cloth,
In a sea of grass.
Castaway kids.

Click-clack heels on the platform,
As your feathered hat
Bobbed its way through the crowd
Towards me.

Furtive moments grabbed from a party.
A toppled ink-well,
Instant Rorschach.

Passing,
In too much haste, unknowing,
On a dusty road between Jos and Kano.

Your deep, deep capacity for enjoyment.
How you could take
A house, a friend, a child,
A book, a film, a pet,
A recipe,
Take them deep into your heart with joy.

How, in the security of your reign,
I knew how it was
To be loved.

Who Said That?

There are some phrases
I now use,
Have to use
Quite frequently,
But,
I don't know what they mean,
Like,
'My wife died recently,'
Or,
'I am a widower.'

Other people know what they mean.
Their expressions change straightaway
To wary,
Watchful,
Sympathetic,
Pained.

Sometimes,
When I mouth and hear those words,
Of widower, wife and dead,
I want to look around
To see who said them.

Some things I understand,
Too well.
Silence,
Solitude,
The stutter of unuttered and unanswered words.
Their emptinesses fill my days.

Others things show more,
By being less.
Warmth would be an example.

But some are new.
That clutch of images.

Those final days.
That night.
That helpless, useless witness
To that last scene,
Which plays and plays,
Putting knots into my breath,
Till I am become an expert in your dying,
Whilst yet a novice from your death.

Moonshadowed

Where are you still lurking?
In tasks we planned to share,
In trips to make,
In a few still-folded shirts,
In choices.
'That lamp,' you insisted,
And that shade of towel,
(My preference overruled).
That brand of olive oil,
So extra virginal
I fear arrest each time I use it.
A shelf of empty jars, for jam.
More shelves,
And drawers
Of strangely spiced ingredients,
All stranded now.
Mail order catalogues
With pages marked.
Shoes,
And more shoes,
And more and more.
The Chinese dress I brought back from Penang,
The bodice made to fit my sculpting hands,
Remembering your breasts.
That sweeping, long, black coat,
Edged with yet blacker, eye-browed, furry opulence.
Medicines,
So many.
Brushes, combs, oils and creams,
Lotions and powders.
How full of business your life was.
Scraps of paper floating up
With messages.
My days' routines,
Which still embody yours.
That new and precious pan
You lost the time to use.

I argued against it
But now use it all the time.
How does an absence make itself so felt,
That not being there gives locus to a thought?
Etched out so deeply from a life that was,
Deep claw-marks on a dragged-down victim's pelt,
Echoes from a battle bravely fought,
A shadow marking still its vanished source,
Each empty dress by swelling memory filled,
Jackets and coats which hold a body's heat,
Trinkets and jewels poised for your careful choice,
From pots and jars your fragrances still spilled,
Sandals and shoes await your searching feet.
I enter a room and listen for your voice.
Moonshadowed into permanent eclipse,
My frozen words chafe at my frozen lips.

Our 5-year Plan.

After Papworth,
After the picture became clear,
The tumour gone
But emphysema rampant,
The dodgy valve
And asthma,
The mad dance with steroids.
After our hopes were up,
Then down,
Then cautious,
We settled for a 5-year plan.
It was, we thought,
A modest aim.
Less modestly perhaps
Renewed from year to year.
Just five more years became
A rolling programme
Lasting twelve.
Yes. We were getting older,
Your slow decline continued,
But, five years went on looking reasonable to us,
Something small enough to hope for,
Low enough on the list of projects for approval,
For whoever was playing God,
To pass it on the nod.
Your life still shone bright,
Even to eyes less prejudiced than mine.
There were things unfinished,
New things yet to do,
Memories to be checked and docketed,
Anecdotes revised, refreshed, retold,
Chronologies unravelled.
But now,
Relieved of my old roles
Of husband, lover, friend,
A mere executor,
There are things I do not know,

That you could tell me.
We lived by rules I have not fathomed yet.
Knowledge has been lost.
The balance of your past,
Not yet transferred to my account.
Already in arrears,
Each day confirms
How desperately I miss and need
Another five good years.

Moping but Coping

When people ask how I am,
I reply,
Jokily brave,
'Moping, but coping.'

I'd like to add,
'Hoping.'
Hoping for hoping.
Geddit?
But what would I hope for?
I'm not certain yet.

No good going straight to the top of the list,
That you'll turn up beside me
In bed,
Or your armchair,
Watching TV,
Fondling the cats,
Or, ensconced in your wheelchair,
Boudicca round the shops,
Or combing the catalogues
For grandchildren's clothes,
Or pressing out pastry,
Or, slowly with scissors
At loose in the garden,
Cropping the flowers.

(The dead heads all thrive now,
If you see what I mean).

If I try hard
Will I find them,
Some sensible hopes?
Twelve hours a day I could put in
Of sensible hoping,
Just time off for lunch.
But what would they be
These sensible hopes?

Not that eyes would stay dry,
Or memories fade,
Or to flee from this place
Where my anguish was made.

I'll start looking tomorrow,
Lots on at the moment.
Long face and self pity
Are keeping me busy.

Sometimes I manage
The bright and the breezy,
But hoping is hard,
While hopeless comes easy.

Advantages

All these things I can do now,
Like,
Listen to Bartok,
Enjoy modern jazz,
Watch and cheer at sport on TV,
Cook and eat kippers,
(No complaints about smell),
Walk over cobbles, or beaches, or mud,
Along paths blocked by lampposts,
Use stairs and not lifts,
All previously banned as wheelchair unfriendly,
Take cable-cars up into cold, air-starved mountains,
Unfit for your lungs,
So clogged and so fragile,
Climb mountain paths,
Trek jungle,
Walk meadows,
Cross stiles,
Explore castles from dungeon to battlement,
No end of a good time.

And then there're the things I no longer need do,
Like,
Listen to chefs on TV, or soaps, or biblical epics.
(I never did watch them, but often could hear them).
I can stop being Superman in the supermarket,
Juggling wheelchair and trolley,
Scanning shelves,
Dodging ankles,
Heeding your cries of, 'Slow down Jim! Slow down!'
I can walk safely past shoe-shops,
Walk into an airport with just one small bag,
Sit by the window,
Make last minute bookings.
I can tell lies.
It would be safe to get drunk.

I could dance at a disco,
Or relax
And be old.
(I ate the nut-clusters in that last box of Black Magic).
The house-name is my choice now,
It is now up to me.
I've won that small battle.
Dying disqualifies.
Just one voter left now.
I find I'm unanimous.

I can sleep in a cold room
With windows wide open,
Leave spiders to roam,
Let cats wait for their food.

I write poems about this.

I can walk out of the house
Without your hand's touch
Straightening my collar,
Or fastening a button,
Or being pulled down
So that your fingers can comb through my hair,
Without your soft scrutiny,
Without your approval,
Sweet-grudgingly given.

So you see!
No end of advantage,
No clutter,
No conflict.
The winner.
No contest.

Please. No more such gifts.
Rich food for the starved
Too grossly will fill me.
More kindness like this,
With kindness will kill me.

Poor at Maths

I've read of men who lived a double life,
A wife in one town, and some children too.
But secretly, elsewhere, another wife
And children. And I've wondered, haven't you?
How do they do it? Always on the brink
Of dire disclosure. The wrong word that slips.
Sex would be the easiest part I think.
Disaster is detail. Birthdays, school-trips,
Knowledge and feelings not allowed to show.
Each orbit shaken by the other's pull.
The panic as the subterfuges grow.
Each life with truth, lies, secrets overfull.
I had one wife. She died. I now have none.
Our doubled life, now halved, leaves less than one.

More is Less.

Yet what remains is like a double life.
I switch between the two in swift disguise.
Most time I spend in routine's placid strife,
But leave it and occasion no surprise.
In thought I flicker to that other scene,
That you inhabit still, both young and old.
Revisit places where we both have been.
Again we are together. No-one scolds
My absence, as old habits write my days.
I walk, and shop, and talk, and drink, and eat,
And, though my head might nod and eyes might glaze,
Even close companions see not that we meet.
Two lives, but purchased at so dear a cost;
Cruel compensation for the one I lost.

I Turn Away

From drifted snow
On hedges curled,
Crouched above your startled head,
Which dodges snowballs, gently hurled,
Fierce snow, which trapped us on the road that night,
But now, by day,
Benignly rumpled, like a bed,
From memories and sights like these
Of us at play,
Each day I turn my face away.

From sights of spring,
With you beside that hovering tree,
Whose leaves so gently brush your face,
On grass, which creeps about your toes,
Where waters glint and ripples race.
Your secret smile which comes and goes.
From sights like these,
From all that precious April day,
I turn away.

From summer scenes
Of sunshine, skipping through your hair,
And sun-bright flowers which catch your eyes,
Whose petals feel your touch,
Whose scent your senses gladly take,
For my senses now too much,
Conniving all my heart to break,
From all of these
I turn away.

From tired autumn's darkening skies
And falling fruit,
October creeping in to cast
Its sudden curse across the fields,
Of all the seasons, this the last
To which I turn,

To which I'm first to yield.
At its approach my hurt still cries.
Grey hours crowd out the shrinking day.
The fearsome holly spurts its blood,
And circling thoughts descend to brood.
From this,
I turn my face away.
My coward's face I turn away.

Holding On

I dreamed I sat beside you.
You were hurting.
I put my arm around you.
You leaned towards me
As you always did.

I dreamed that we had troubles,
Trivial, but a bother.
You said that you would sort them,
As you always did.

I dreamed I phoned your office.
You were not there,
But, someone went in search.
They said you'd soon return and phone me back.
You always did.

I did not tell them you were dead.
I said I'd wait.
I hoped the dream was strong,
That they would find you,
As they always had.

Detained under Section 18b of the Dental Health Act.

Some people, I suspect,
Wish I would stop.
Stop writing poems that is.
Or, at least, poems like these.
(And it's not just poetry-lovers I'm talking about).

'Time passes,' they say.
'Time heals,' they claim.
'Life moves on,'
'A new life begins,'
'The pain will go.'
'In time you will look back without grief,'
'But with a kind of gentle, almost pleasant, melancholy.'
'The past will become like a slowly decaying tooth'
'That will hurt only if you prod it.'

'You will prod it of course,'
'Because, by then, the pain will have become a friend.'
'But you will find new friends,'
'And then, a touch of Novocaine,'
'The briefest tug and,'
'No more prodding, no more pain,'
'Just a gap,'
'And you are yourself again.'

Their logic grates,
And, as memory's searching tongue
That gap anticipates,
'What self would that be, that was left?' I wonder,
'Should this poor, but now familiar, not-myself, go under?'

The Cottage in the Woods

Sometimes
The past is like a house of treasure
Left unguarded.
I rummage,
Heap my arms high
With artful, heartful artefacts,
Till my bones ache,
And memory bursts, from all this booty,
Beauty,
Leaking its tears down unstroked cheeks.
Other times,
The past is a cottage in the woods,
With me outside,
Looking wistfully through glass
At a remembered tableau.
A group, gathered round the fire,
Wearing their lives like comfortable clothes,
Their future, an invitation, propped on the mantle-piece.
In a corner a baby sleeps,
Burns like a small furnace,
Warming the house.
Wind, complaining and brutal,
Elbows its blustering way through the darkness behind me.
Thumps at my back, rattling the glass.
The baby startles,
Then settles more deeply.
Family figures look out at the storm.
(My younger face is there, amongst them).
They smile in grateful triumph,
Savouring their comfort.
One of them shivers and stares.
Is that face mine?
Did I sense out there,
Out here,
One faint howl amongst the louder howlings,
Distinctive as a baby's cry,
Stirring the cords in my throat,
Tracing its cool tune along my spine?

A Little Touch of Wolfitt in the Night.

I rage about the empty house,
A major act in every room,
A final scene, slumped in my chair,
Pronouncing doom.

No audience though,
My movements to admire and cheer,
Or sad soliloquies applaud to hear,
Just echoing space,
And startled cats,
And dislodged mats.

Just fifty years ago
One rented room held all my fantasies,
A museum case of, mainly, nothingness.
My one man show.
A pile of books upon an empty bed.

Now, in this house, of you but recently so full,
That same exhibit, thinly spread,
Aspires to fill nine rooms, a double-garage and a swimming-pool.

The stranded actor mouths forgotten lines,
Each speech a bluster and each move a blunder.
A relic glaring from its prison case,
A face of frantic thunder.

Voice Training.

No need to shout.
No need to scream.
A voice can gain edge
From a passing dream.

Memory's a rock,
To sharpen, or break.
Cracked notes run amok
To drive you awake.

Love gave balm.
Death brought pain.
None of your songs
Will please her again.

Something in the City

Another dream.

You in that business suit
You learned to wear.
So smart.
White blouse collar up,
Framing tidy hair.

We laughed,
As though your being an accountant
Was a glorious sexy game.
You as city girl strippergram,
Sent as a wondrous, silly gift,
To lift,
Not just my spirits.

Hands-held, we ran across a road,
Your breathing easy then, as once it was.
'I feel so good!' you said.
Your attention was upon me.
We hugged and kissed for joy
And, for a blissful while before I woke,
We spoke.

Double Vision

I look in the garden.
What do I see?
A tree.

Before the garden,
In the glass,
Before the tree,
A watchful me.

Before my picture in the glass,
Before the tree,
And garden too,
A shade of you.

I put my hands upon my eyes.
As remedy, it works quite well.
Crushing the snail back in its shell,
I squeeze until the darkness breaks,
Banishing garden, tree and you and me,
Till brain and hands and elbows ache.

Damp hands fall, shaking, to my sides.
The mind its function re-asserts.
Far and near, things re-appear.
Tree and garden come anew.
The glass again shows me and you.
Now and then re-claim the view,
Refuse to hide,
And soon, again, the looking hurts.

I Had Not Thought

I had not thought that pain could last so long.
I had not thought so many tears could fall.
I had not thought that grief could be so strong.
I had not thought at all.

The Wary Traveller.

There are places I can't visit.
We were there.
Your ghost still hovers.
A cafe table, a sea-side seat,
A side-show at a fair.

There are places I can't go because,
Because we planned to go,
But didn't.
Business left undone,
I cannot do alone.

There are places I can't go,
Which you would not have chosen, but,
I like the sound of them.
The worry here for me is,
Can I be so free?

Further down that street,
Lurk deeper shadows yet.
People I might meet,
I never would have met.

Hereafter.

As witness to your final breath,
Birth pangs to an after-life,
(Life does continue after death,
As when a man outlives his wife),

This other world is strange to me.
The person I was I still resemble.
People I knew I still can see,
As friends and family assemble.

And yet, there is a difference,
Like voices from another room.
I listen to their dialogue.
I hear it pause, and then resume.

Your death, my life, a harsh disjunction.
Something you have lost I keep.
A sort of life without a function,
Except, perhaps, to mourn, and weep.

The ghost that walks about the house
Inhabiting our favourite places,
Walks only when I am around,
Wears one of my forgotten faces.

Museum Pieces.

I once had, in my parents' house,
A small collection of rough drawings, scribbles, doodles,
Left from a summer when I thought I might become an artist.
The summer wasn't long enough, they never are,
But I'd be curious to see those dabblings now,
Small pictures by (and therefore of) myself, as then.
When I left home, I put them in a trunk.
It was made of tin, but tin got up to look like wood, or maybe leather,
With imitation bolt-heads pressed from the metal.
At their last house-move, it disappeared.
My drawings and my collection of shrapnel from the war,
Razor shapes, base plates, nose cones,
Harvested from morning pavements like seashore gleanings,
All lost, or casually abandoned,
Left behind by those I loved.

A later move......... more casualties .... missing in action.
My old army shirt, old baggy football shorts,
A collection of park-keepers' hats purloined from holiday jobs,
Snow clearing, leaf burning,
Cleaning graffitti (once I'd read them) from toilets (Gents and Ladies),
Momentoes of bothie breakfasts,
Of housewives at the further reaches of the park,
Popping out from their pre-fabs, to offer cups of tea.
Four or five of those hats I'd collected,
High crowned, brown and sturdy.
We used them for waste paper bins about the house, and fancy dress.
Mysteriously gone.
Quietly, with secret glee, conspiratorially abandoned.
Brimful of memories, but left behind, by those I loved.

At your final moving on,
A whole house is now abandoned.
Full still of clothes, cosmetics, shoes,
Wools and cottons, brushes,
Which I can barely touch, or look at,
But do not throw away.

Relics of weddings, birthdays, deaths,
Travels and travails,
Sprawled uncomfortably about like debris from an auction,
De-valued now the bidders have gone home.
I too, among the wreckage, part of the jetsam,
I feel de-valued too, and wonder...
'Was there some reserve, some asking price, I failed to meet,'
'To be abandoned so, and left behind,'
'By one I loved?'

Unsafe Haven

It's months since I took this walk.
The churned earth has since been planted,
Borne green shoots and tall gold stems;
Been cropped, and churned afresh.
The puddles look the same,
Joined up to leave concrete islands,
Margins of mud.
The burnt-out car still rots and rusts.
I have been churned and churned again,
Bruised to the roots,
Rotted and rusted,
But, bear no green shoots.

At the turn of the road,
There, at the field's highest hump,
Appears a button, which becomes a small bump,
A chimney, then a roof, and windows too,
Glinting with evening sun,
As my steady pace gradually pulls them into view.
I have walked and walked, and thought,
But my thoughts touch nothing new.

Then, as I turn from the lane,
Evading the windy branches and wet leaves,
There is the house, our house.
We chose it together.
It sits, warm and welcoming,
Plump with our books.
Lights shine. There is music....
And voices.
Coats hang, heaped upon hooks.
Yours is amongst them.
'Do not, do not,' I tell myself, 'Assume,'
As I step through the door, to find
The TV playing to an empty room.

The Trouble Is.

The trouble is,
I cannot yet believe,
Though many months have past,
Though I have learned to grieve,
And though the pain is vast....

The trouble is,
That though I know you've gone,
Yet if you did return,
That shock would still be less
Than the one I face each dawn.

My problem is,
That Science I'd renounce,
Logic and Knowledge too,
Were my senses to announce
That what I saw was you.

The problem is
I still expect to find,
Defying every rule,
That fate will yet be kind,
Which so far has been cruel.

Truth does not set me free,
But nurtures my confusion.
The wrench of you from me
Has left a huge contusion,
And that my trouble is.

Exit Interview

In the course of my career
I became multi-skilled.
Over the years, I'd learned how to give pleasure,
Delay, tease, then detonate, explode.
I could also entertain,
Make jokes. Not tell them but,
With a word, a walk, a look,
An accent or expression,
Draw your laughter, wry amusement,
A knowing grin, a giggle,
Or helpless begging, 'Stop! Oh stop! Oh please stop Jim!'
I could cook, wash clothes, clean carpets,
Shop, plan holidays,
Negotiate with doctors,
With receptionists even.
I learned to take care.
I knew your interests and aversions,
Your tastes, which meals you liked to cook
And which to eat.
Which memories you treasured most,
Which tales you liked to tell and which to hear,
Which photos show.

I could still contrive surprise.
We played our conversational duets,
Could spot each other's lies,
Were audience and performers,
Gave and received applause,
Might make a bow and take a curtain call.

Going solo,
As you've guessed,
Is not such fun at all.

Disconnections.

Things I touch
Click sometimes, sometimes rudely, into action,
Fetch messages.

Out there,
My service provider holds them,
Till, even if randomly, a right button does get pressed.

To turn away too suddenly
Can cause cosmic consternation.
I am told I have performed an illegal operation.

Once, I knew which buttons to press
To provide or receive service,
To set bells jangling in the cellar.

Needs,
Save for some dalliance,
Were attended to promptly.

The House of the Dead.

My wife's tomb
Has many mansions.

One for the joyous shouts of her youngest.
Their wispy memories flick at her lightly
As they choose.

One for those who knew her only for a while, but well,
Who clutch bright jewels of close remembrances
They will never wish to lose.

One for those who knew her best and longest,
Who dust and trace and cherish old, friendly shapes,
As from the mind's jumble, they arise.

One is a narrow room of hellfire cold and burning ice,
For he who cannot hold, or purge, or sleep, or wake, or work, or rest,
Imprisoned by those eyes.

Nothing Purrsonal.

I'm having problems with one of our cats,
Puzzled that, though sitting in your chair,
I do not continue your affection.
He keeps demanding to be treated like a person,
As you treated him in fact.
He thinks he's my friend,
Anticipates mealtimes,
Lots of mealtimes,
(14 times a day he trots expectantly before me),
Tries luring me into walks,
Helps in the garden,
Strikes up conversations,
Presents me with mice,
Watches me endlessly,
Studies my moods and movements,
Purrs mightily,
Given half a chance, would climb onto my lap,
Knead me with sharp, soft paws,
Then drool and bite,
And has a look of calm intelligence
Upon his wise, cat-handsome face,
But, on one topic, he is somewhat dim,
Is not bright enough to see that,
In my life,
Though empty,
Is no room for him.

And a Happy New Year

'Christmas is a sad time,'
So the poet said.
'For a range of reasons,'
'People cry in bed.'

I find sadness permanent,
Not seasonal, or yearly.
The fairy lights of Christmas
Just show it up more clearly.

Tired in the Bone

Tired in the bone,
And in my brain,
I leave the ward,
Towards home again.

Tired in my bones,
And in my heart and blood,
I sit in the car. Let tears trickle,
Soon to flood.

Tired in my bones,
And in my ears and eyes,
That have watched your pain,
And heard your cries.

Tired in my bones,
As scenes re-appear.
The quieter your calls,
The louder my fear.

Home through the dark
To kettle and cup.
Phone calls and letters
To prop spirits up.

Those times passed,
Leaving their wound,
But left you alive,
With me, above ground.

Grateful years
To cherish each day,
Till death doubled back,
Rejoined our play.

Fate moved fast,
Left me alone,
Harrowed and haunted,
Tired in the bone.

A Sailor's Life for Me.

Not able again to share a home,
I'll buy a boat and learn to roam.
Read a bit, abstain from sport,
And look for a lovely lady,
A lovely, lonely lady,
In each port.

Double Glazed.

I see trees toss, flail, bend under blows,
But cannot hear their sighs.
Watch clouds crowd swift, dark and silent to a distant point,
As though to terrorise.
See, but not hear, the furious squabbling of birds
As they strut and bounce between lawn and scowling skies.

Can they see me?
Observe my tears?
But hear me not?
Not hear my cries?

Do they wonder why?

'No,' hoots an owl,
From a nearby fence.
'Birds, by and large, are somewhat dense.'
'And the rest, like myself,'
'Have too much sense.'
'Try an emetic.'
'Your fallacy's pathetic.'

Anniversary Song.

There are times when
I feel so hungry for human contact
I am afraid that it will show,
Perhaps like a green film, surfacing my skin,
Or a tendency to spark at handshakes, hugs or fleeting kisses,
Or that my arms will tighten,
Lips drink more than convention sanctions,
Feet take me too close for the other's comfort,
That my body, desert dry,
Yet, will suck like quicksand,
Eyes, like dying bonfires,
Stirred by secret winds,
Will flash alarmingly with meaning,
As, leper-like,
With silenced bell,
I pace the eleventh spiral
Of this third year hell.

Abbeygayle.

The cemetery,
Which we did not know of in your life,
Has a centre path.
Regular Christians one side, on the right,
Other denominations and unbelievers on the left.
Even in death, there are choices to be made.

I visited once, before the funeral,
Sampled its quiet heart,
Ribbed round with the distant hum of traffic,
Football shouts,
A Hoover in the nearest bungalow.

The path forks, leaving a central plot.
These headstones smaller, crowded closer,
A place of ashes.

Your last drive took you through the town.
A parade of heads. Some turned.
Others too busy living to look up.

The hearse whispered over pebbles,
Our feet shuffling in broken step behind.
Our destination an intrusion of earth,
Bruising the Fenland sky.
Boards placed blatantly above a raw, fresh trench.

A hastily devised rough service....
Wet words, proud poems,
Throats torn by tributes and tears,
The rattle of stones.

Back at the house, more talk,
Photos, friends and food.
Sorrow enlarged and eased.

On my next visit
It was as though the earth,
Like a warm, brown bear
Had crept back into its lair,
Covering itself with a quilt of flowers.

Later again, the flowers were gone,
Bare earth settled,
Bright blades of grass advancing,
Healing the scar.

At each further visit,
With my small bunch of flowers,
I find the last bouquet is neatly nibbled down.
By deer? Or rabbits?
This would please you.
I imagine your smile
To hear their soft, pit-pat approach,
Your hands gently rustling the stems,
Lips pursed into softest kissing,
To tempt them nearer.

No headstone yet.
I cannot choose the words.
Yet, everyday, at home, in poems, words do come.

Halfway between where you lie
And the gate, where, coming in, I collect water in a plastic jug,
And going out drop stagnant stalks and weeds in the dumper–skip,
Surrounded by messages of hope for peace,
Assurances of reunions and future joys,
On stones in memory of William, Henry, Frederick, Martha, Joan,
Margaret and Patricia,
A bare white cross, close-crowded to the path,
Nervous before the others,
Like a reluctant child, pushed to the front
For a family photo,
Weathered and pale,
Much smaller than the rest,

With one date only,
Like a milestone on my journey,
I pass the grave of Abbeygayle.

And from this point,
For fifty paces more,
I fill my mind with Abbeygayle.

The greater loss to lose a child.
The greater pain, the greater grief,
The more unfair the tragedy,
The anger and the disbelief.

But then, I reach your side and know
There is no greater pain than this,
No huger gulf, more deep abyss,
Regrets to nurse, despair to show.
A simple truth to learn this late,
That grief we cannot calibrate.

Retracing now my former trail,
With memories and last week's flowers,
I pass again, now on my left,
The tiny grave of Abbeygayle.

On every stone there is a name.
All are different, all the same.

In every cross there is a nail,
In every grave an Abbeygayle.

They're Coming!

Busy to the last,
Though trapped by sheets,
Attached to tubes,
Propped
And foully bloated,
You scattered tiny smiles like petals
Round the ward,
Began weak conversations,
Welcomed new arrivals,
Gave them the dope on doctors,
Know-how on nurses,
Reassured with praise for their care,
Greeted visitors and calmed their fears.

Even later,
As I dabbed cooled water on hot lips, flushed cheeks,
Around grateful eyes,
Even as I was eased beyond the curtains,
Banished your bedside,
To kick heels,
Stare at shelves,
Shrug off the comfort of professional arms,
Pace corridors,
Howl silently at lunar-lights,
Fumble the phone with midnight summonses,
As I cursed and swore and begged in rigid silence,
I could hear your gasping jokes
To your sorry saviours,
Brave thanks for failure.

Imagined your eyes caught by a fluttering pennant,
The flick of reins, and clink of cutlasses,
The creak of leather,
Brim-blown hats,
The sweat of horses,
The trumpet and its rescue call,
The furious approach, then gradual fading, of thunderous hooves
As they galloped away and beyond
Down another valley.

Fire Sale – Everything Must Go.

In a shop window,
I see a reflection
Of an old man,
Limping,
Badly,
And think,
'That's not me.'

At another viewing the limp is worse,
And, I notice lips pressed tight,
To dampen pain.
Lips which then loosen to mouth the words,
'Not me. Not me.'

Nor me is that slow, hobbling movement,
And the fact that he walks alone.

Later,
In the fire,
Are other pictures.
Children scampering on a beach.
Sheepdog parents laughing at their heels.

I see a figure
Bouncing a baby on a pain-free knee,
Hovering to help an older man
Who learns to walk with sticks,
Running with dextrous heed
Behind your wheel-chair.

As the coals settle,
In the fire's deep heart,
I see two bodies,
Shimmering flames,
Which touch and merge,
Then pull apart,
Then touch and merge again.

I see those burning bodies
Shooting sparks,
Convulsed, consumed,
Shedding hot tears,
Which sizzle into steam,
And sigh,
'That's me.'
'That's me.'

The Last Taboo.

I heard it again the other day,
That confident, smug assertion,
'Death is the Last Taboo,'
Which is beginning to sound
Suspiciously like a cliché,
Trotted out in place of thought.
Perhaps thought is the last taboo.
Yes, some of my most comfortable thoughts are cliches,
But what does this one mean?
The speaker, it implies,
Knows how we should behave,
If someone dies.
And thinks that we
Are not dealing with it properly.
Like Ofsted-inspected teachers,
Reduced to fools,
Hearing that same, sad song.
'All you are doing is wrong,'
Or, 'Could be done better.'
'And is done better,'
'In another country,'
'In some far-off schools.'
'Look at that lot,' these Taboo-artists seem to say,
'They weep and wail and tear their hair,'
'Try to jump into the grave, enjoy despair.'
'Couldn't you do something in that line?'
'Show some flair?'
But, who does know how to deal with death?
How to lose a wife, a child, a mother?
And what would make that way more proper?
Can any way, anyway,
Be more proper than another?
Most times we stumble into death.
We thrash about.
Cope, after a fashion.
Speak, or are silent.
Cry, or are stuck, dry-eyed, with buried passion,

90

Remember, or forget.
Recover, or go under.
Catch ourselves laughing like a drain,
Or fear that we may never laugh again.
Find new love,
Or know that love has died.
Make a new life,
Or lock and lose ourselves inside the old.
Or, more likely,
In our own way and time,
Do all of these,
But clumsily.

Death is clumsy,
Also a muddle.
Sometimes soggy-eyed, snot-nosed, crumpled,
Sometimes cold, clear, tight, a private rage.
Death is personal, made social,
Also a puzzle,
But with no solution
Written upside down at the bottom of the page.
But death a taboo?
What would you have us do?
What feelings have, words say,
Clothes wear, or funeral dance perform?
And, why should we conform
To what would most suit you?
What would you have us do?
Death leaves us too busy with our grief
To bother with taboo.
Taboo for who?
For me? For you?
Those who talk taboo
Exclude themselves,
Mean me and you.
Death is bigger than taboo.
It hurts. It lasts.
It kills survivors,
Sabotages speech,
Swamps thought.

The throat is clogged,
Breath sticky.
The tongue and tonsils swell,
The brain is swollen too.

But this is common knowledge,
Not taboo.
We suffer in crowds, and solitude,
From neglect, and excess fuss,
There's too much, and too little talk,
Nothing is quite right for us.
We are swept by feelings,
Sometimes false and sometimes true.
Have tortured nights, days torn apart,
And twisted guts, and bursting heart,
And spasmed muscles clenched till black and blue,
But not taboo.
Spare us.
Ask not, et cetera, et cetera,
Prepare yourself.
It comes for you.

I Lift Up Mine Eyes Unto The Lawn.

The garden is still, after the storm.
Mole-hills and tumbled pots,
Dust-bin lids and tilted chairs,
All dressed in snow.

The birds have been fed,
And have gone.
For a while, this space is mine.
I salute, in turn, the oak,
The apple, the tall fir,
The new, not-yet-silvered birches.
The lawn, a fresh, white page,
Awaits my words and thoughts.

Age, and iced-up flagstones,
Put me, the would-be-silent witness,
Under threat, as I stand,
Regaining breath and balance,
Like a fugitive, escaped from the house
And all its business.

Breathing now calm, I stay,
Quiet, but alert.
Poised, but for what?

In this brief pause in life's attack,
Is this the time to unlock memories?
To welcome you back?

A Road Remembered

First came knowledge,
Then, a meteorite-strike of hit-and-miss emotions.
Oceans stirred.
Then came thought.

Between the breakers and the troughs,
Somehow,
A time for thought.
Anticipations.

'What does this mean?'
'What will I do?'

My most persistent thought was that I would stride out
Into the darkness of the night,
And keep on walking,
Like Dickens, quenching, or nursing his demons
On the streets of London,
Walk myself into exhaustion.

But,
Exhaustion's wave came first.
And there were things to do.
Comfort to take,
A formula to follow.

And so, I did not walk,
Not then,
But,
Many dreams since,
A white road unreels before me.
Dark margins loom,
Then pass.
And in the mornings
My feet are tired.

Chaos Theory

With days to go,
Still you dieted,
Trimmed nails,
Moisturised your skin.

Hours before,
You sought cool comfort from a wetted flannel,
Enjoyed the shock of fresh, clean sheets,
Could whisper smiles.

Minutes before,
Each breath sweet respite,
Hands tasted touch.
I finger-combed hair carefully above your ears,
Cheek pressed cheek,
Tears met tears.

With seconds only,
In the rush,
As urgency became emergency,
What then?

Was it a wish,
That the resuscitating team would thin,
Allow this banished face back in?

What thought?
What final thought?
Warp speeded to what cherished corner of the past?

A birth?
A meeting?
One joyful shudder?
Which fitting to be last?
All now slipping,
Like a silken scarf,
Beyond your grasp.

Did you then wonder,
'Does anything matter?'
'Does any one thing now,'
'Lead to any one thing else?'

Take your rest,
But know that, yes,
It did.
It does.

Whether from old life closing down,
Or new life unfurled,
That last beat
Of butterfly breath,
Unleashed chaos on the world.

Dahlia Days.

Remember the dahlias?
They're still growing well.
I let them take their chances with the frost,
But, so far, they've survived.

Dahlias came with the house, in London.
They grew so well on clay
We assumed they wouldn't take to the chalk we moved to next.
But here,
Whether it's the surface silt,
Or deeper sand,
It seems to suit them.

Big golden heads,
Sculpted, multi-coloured mauves and whites,
Tiny buttons,
Bronzes, yellows, reds,
They flourish.
Assert themselves above weeds,
Compete with comfrey,
Brighten the slow deaths of autumn.

They've had no true gardener's care,
No special help from me,
But, sometimes, beyond deserving, things go well,
Not forever,
But for a good long while,
Go well,
Sometimes extraordinarily well,
Sometimes,
For a while.